Claim it, its FREE!

Like free stuff? So do I! Come check out the site and get yourself some freebies!

www.outrageouskatie.com/free

Oh Yes!

The Showdown of 2016.
Any time I hear or see either of these two faces I can't do anything but shake my head in shame.
I look at it this way..
At the end of the day, whoever wins, we ALL lose. HA!
Have fun coloring these faces in or just crossing them out!
Then find and follow me on:

Twitter- @OutrageousKatie
Facebook- Outrageous Katie
Instagram- @OutrageousKatie

Much love from yours truly-

Outrageous Katie

Copyright © 2016 by Swear Word Coloring Book Group

ALL RIGHTS RESERVED. By purchase of this book, you have been licensed one copy for personal use only. No part of this work may be reproduced, use or redistributed in any form or by any means without prior written permission of the publisher and copyright owner.

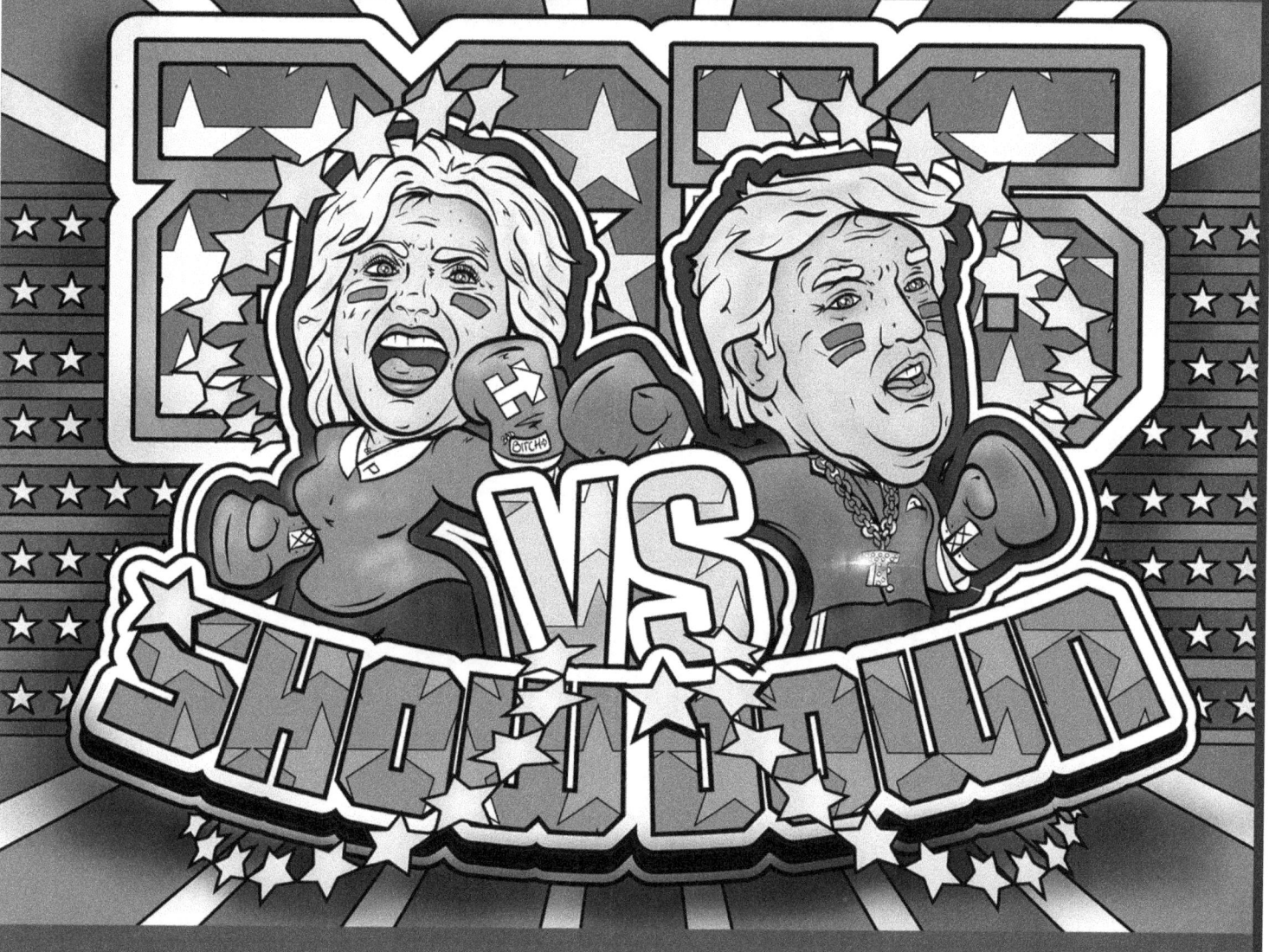

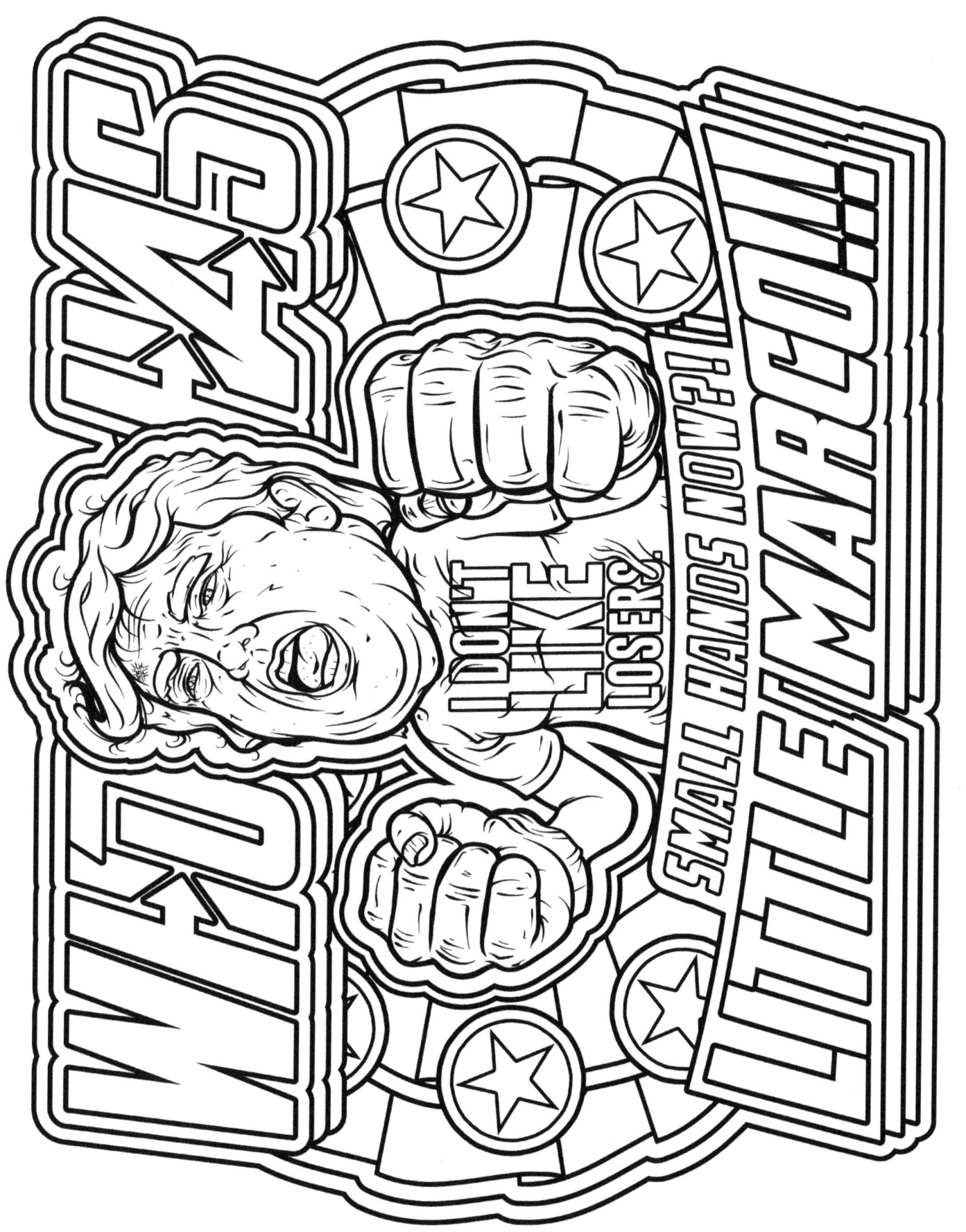

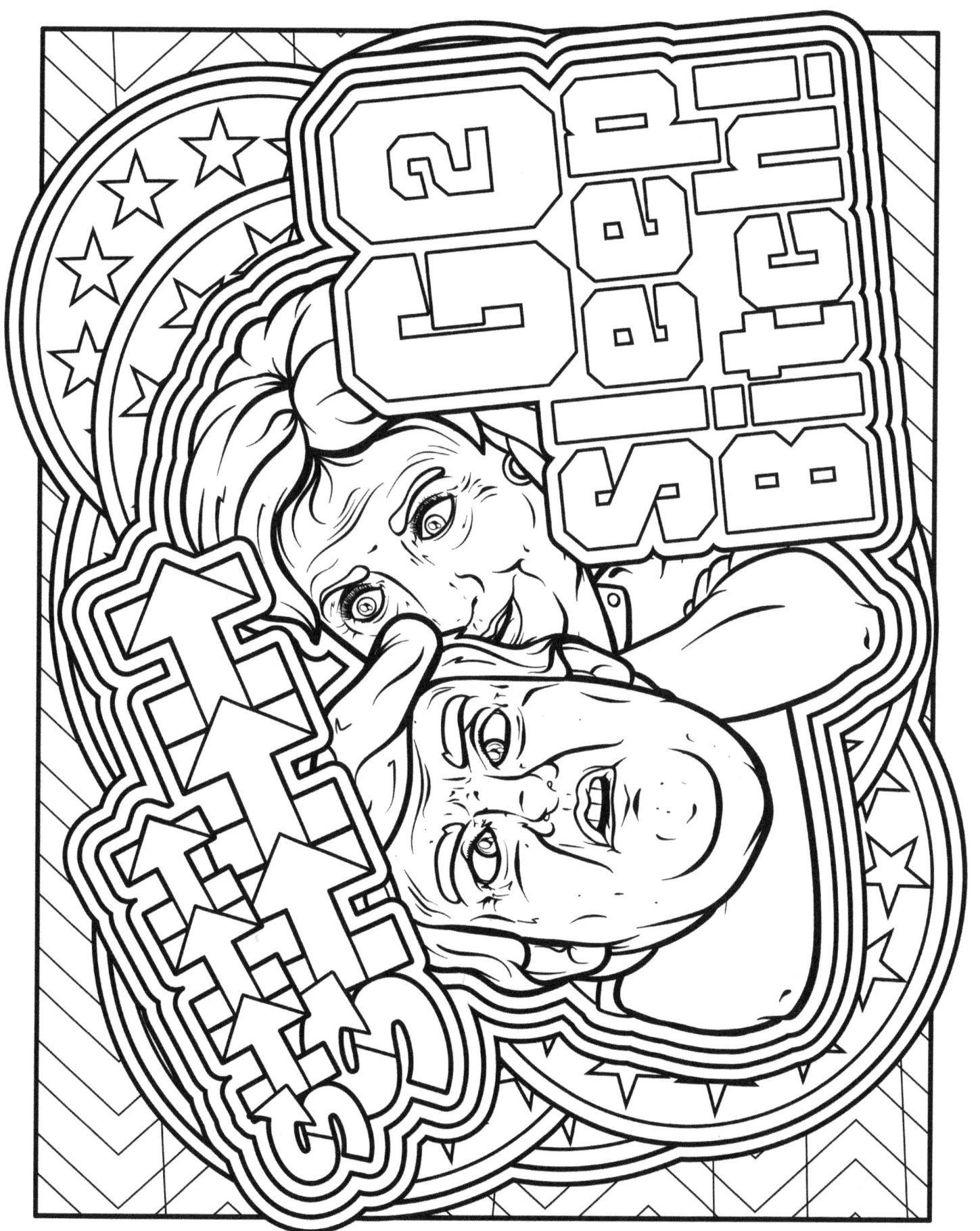

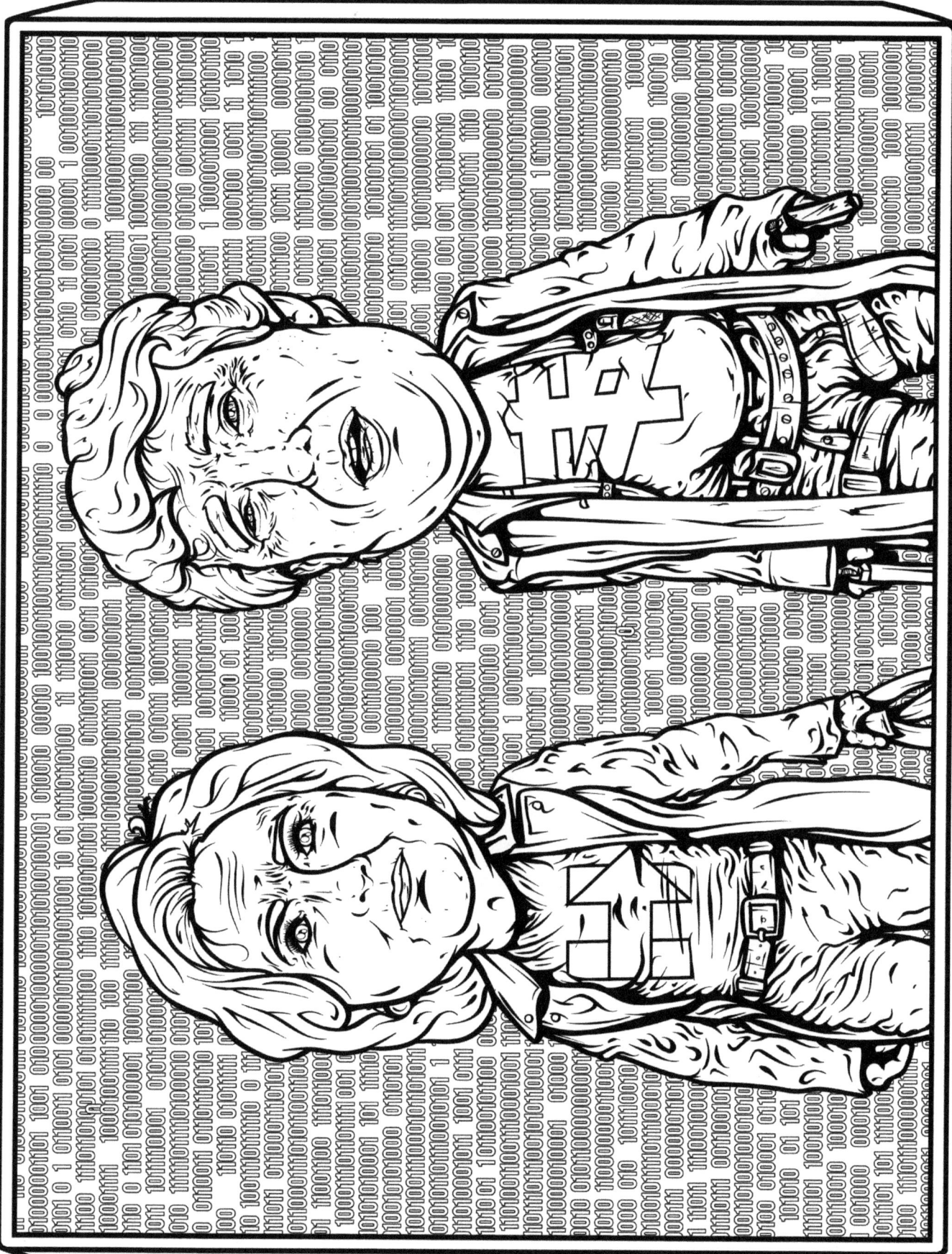

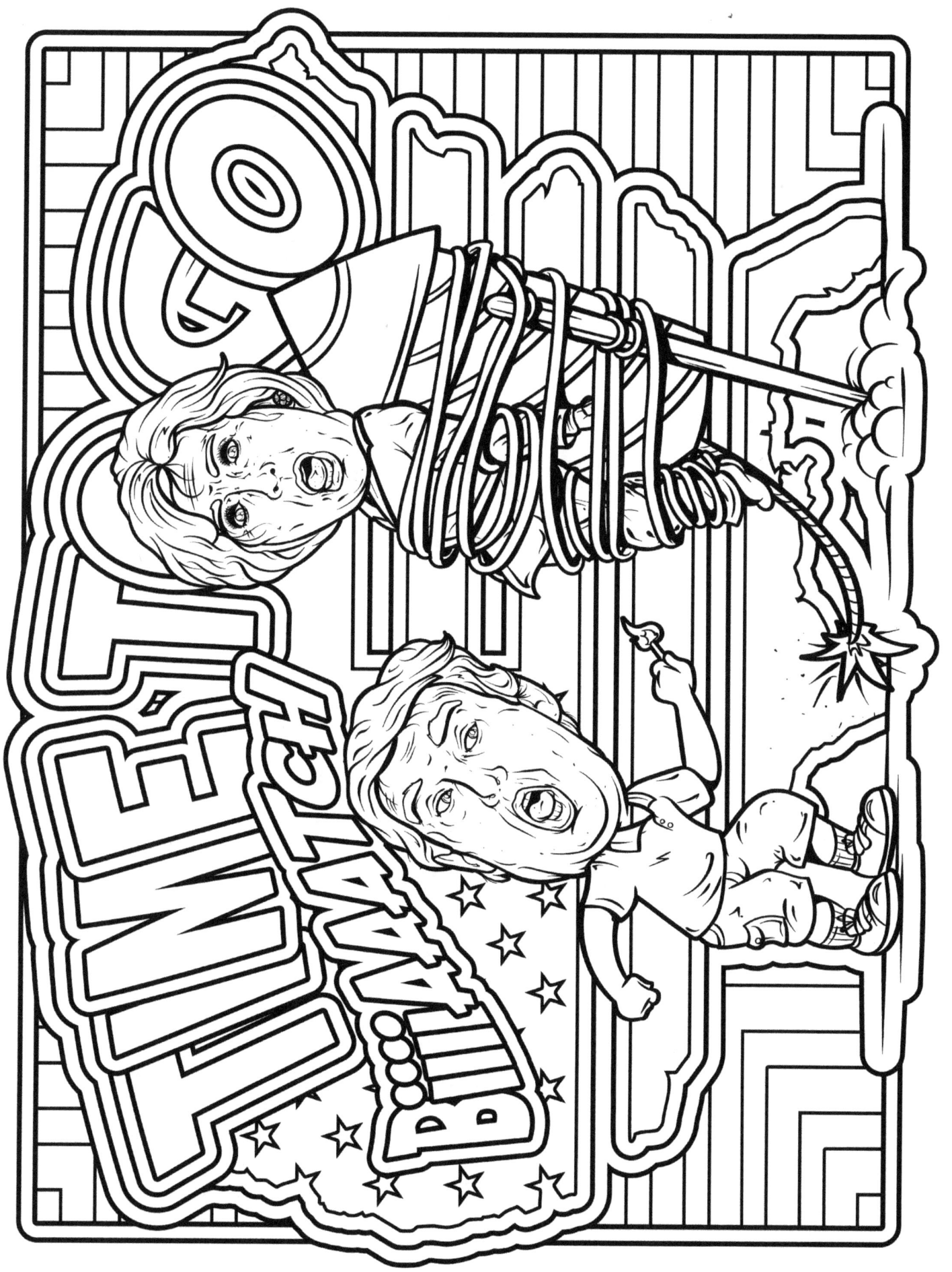

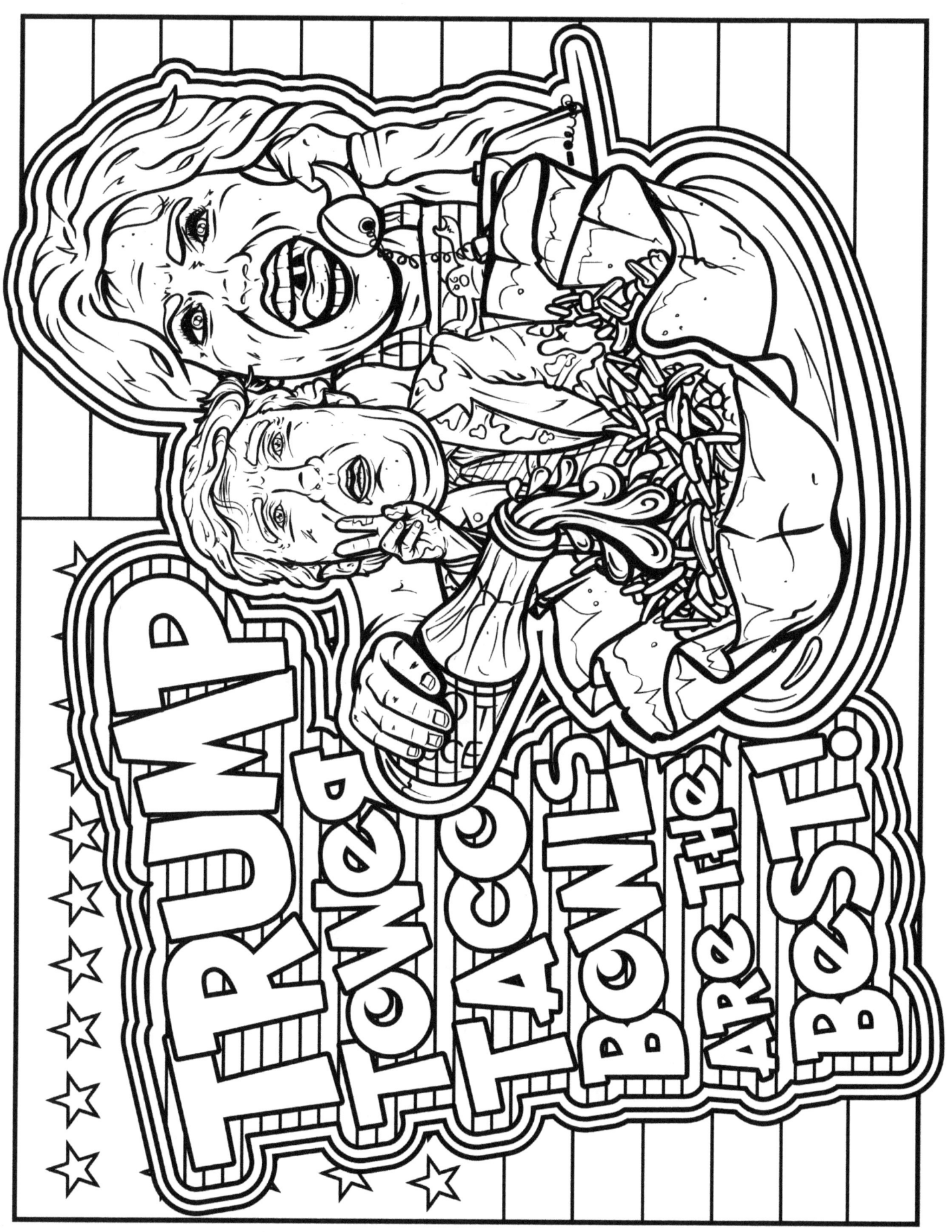

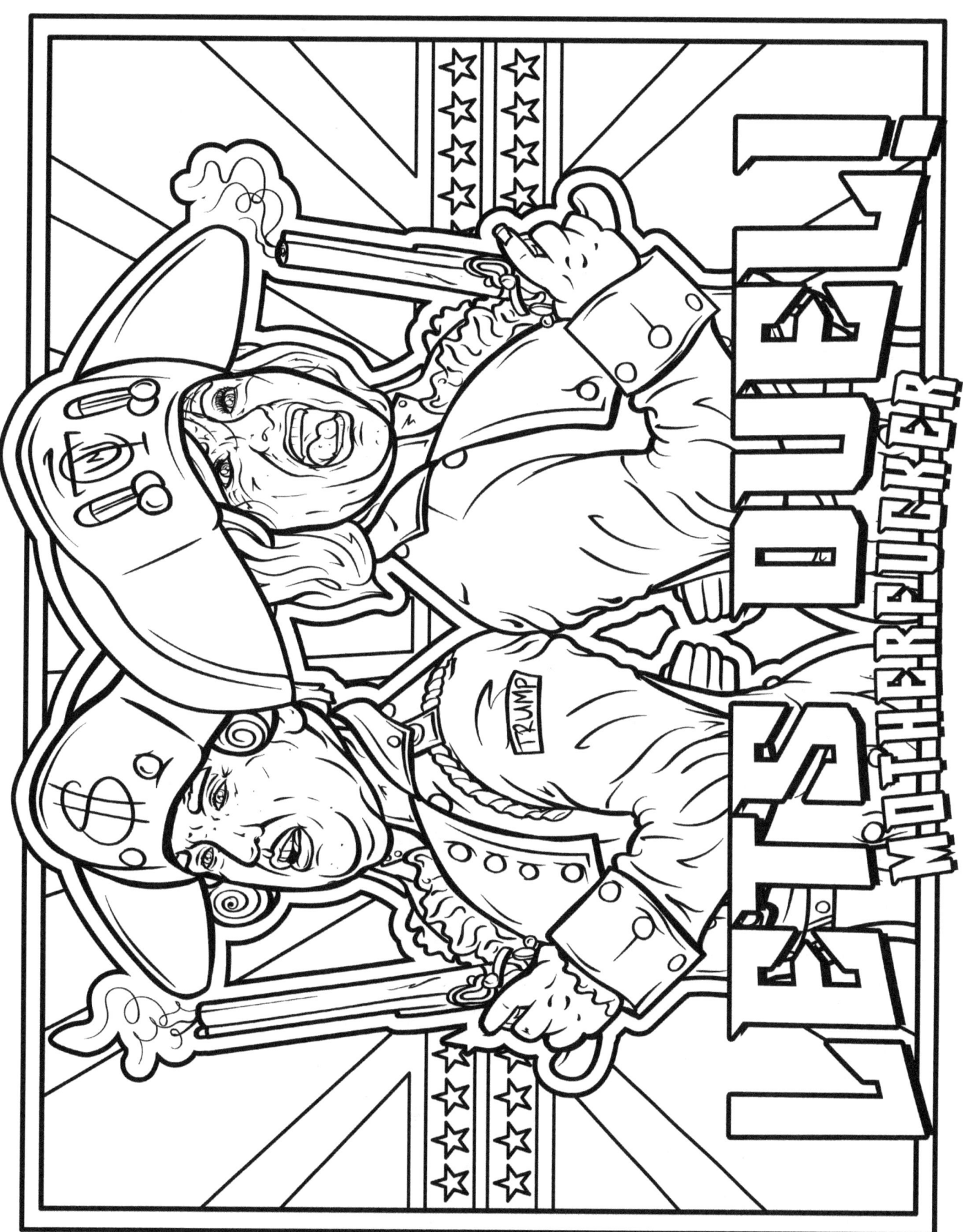

www.ingramcontent.com/pod-product-compliance
Lightning Source LLC
Chambersburg PA
CBHW081254040426
42453CB00014B/2406